MW00961250

Don Lemon:

From Small-Town Roots To National News Anchor(Biography)

Eva M. Cole

Don Lemon

Don Lemon

TABLE OF CONTENTS

Don Lemon

Don Lemon

INTRODUCTION

American journalist and television news host Don Lemon. He was born in Baton Rouge, Louisiana, USA, on March 1, 1966. Lemon received a broadcast journalism degree from Brooklyn College in New York City. At the Fox affiliate in New York City, WNYW, he started off as a news assistant.

Before joining CNN in 2006, Lemon worked as a journalist for NBC News and an anchor for a number of regional stations. He has had a variety of positions at CNN, including news anchor, correspondent, and host of "CNN Tonight with Don Lemon."

Lemon has covered a variety of significant news events over the course of his career, including Hurricane Katrina, Michael Jackson's passing, the Boston Marathon bombing, and the 2016 U.S. presidential election. He has also been an outspoken supporter of social justice, speaking out against topics like racism, police brutality, and LGBTQ+ rights.

Don Lemon

Journalism by Don Lemon is renowned for being honest and occasionally provocative. He has drawn both praise and criticism for his willingness to challenge his guests with difficult questions. Additionally, Lemon has been transparent about his personal encounters with racism and homophobia, which he wrote about in his book "Transparent."

Lemon has made guest appearances on a number of television shows in addition to his employment at CNN, including "The Daily Show with Jon Stewart" and "The Late Show with Stephen Colbert." In addition, he has received numerous honors for his work, including an Emmy for his 2009 coverage of Barack Obama's inauguration.

In addition, Lemon has received praise for his advocacy activities. For his coverage of the BP oil spill, he was given the Journalist of the Year award by the National Association of Black Journalists in 2011. He has

Don Lemon

additionally received recognition from the Human Rights
Campaign for his support of LGBTQ+ rights.

Don Lemon is a well-known journalist and television
news host who has reported on significant news events
and promoted social justice. He is known and respected
in the media world for his candid and forthright
approach to journalism.

CHAPTER 1: EARLY LIFE AND EDUCATION

Don Lemon was born in Baton Rouge, Louisiana, on March 1st, 1966. With three siblings, he grew up in a working-class home. Lemon's father was a businessman who operated a pub, and his mother was a nurse. Growing up, Lemon was exposed to the good times and bad, including segregation, racism, and poverty, that the Black community in the South experienced.

Lemon went to Baker High School in Baton Rouge, where he participated in student government and the debate team. He studied broadcast journalism at Louisiana State University after graduating from high school. Lemon received useful knowledge and exposure to the media sector while working as a news assistant at WNYW in New York City throughout his undergraduate studies.

Don Lemon

Lemon started his career in media as a reporter and anchor at WCAU-TV in Philadelphia after receiving his degree from LSU in 1988. After that, he worked at stations in Chicago, Illinois, and St. Louis, Missouri, before relocating to New York City to work for NBC News.

Early journalism experiences gave Lemon exposure to the media's ability to influence public opinion and create awareness of significant issues. He developed a passion for challenging the existing quo and using his platform to promote social justice. This drive finally brought him to CNN, where he rose to become one of the most well-known and regarded newscasters in the business.

Don Lemon encountered various difficulties relating to his race and sexuality in the early years of his journalism career. Lemon has freely discussed the racism and persecution he has experienced throughout his life and work as a gay Black man. Lemon discusses the difficulties he encountered while growing up in the South in his book "Transparent," including incidents of racism and homophobia. He also talks about how these encounters have influenced his viewpoint as a journalist and social justice activist.

Despite these obstacles, Lemon remained adamant about pursuing a career in journalism and using his position to raise awareness of problems impacting underrepresented groups of people. His devotion and hard work paid off, and he advanced swiftly in the business.

Lemon began working for CNN as a correspondent and anchor in 2006. He has hosted a number of shows for the network over the years, including "CNN Newsroom," "CNN Tonight," and "Don Lemon Tonight." Additionally, he has frequently contributed to CNN's coverage of significant news events, including the COVID-19 outbreak and the 2016 U.S. presidential election.

Three Emmy achievements, as well as recognition from the National Association of Black Journalists and the National Association of Lesbian and Gay Journalists, are just a few of the honors and achievements Lemon has received for his work at CNN. On-air and off-air, he has developed a reputation for his outspoken advocacy on matters of race, sexuality, and social justice.

Overall, Don Lemon's upbringing and education lay the groundwork for both his journalism profession and his ardent commitment to the causes of underprivileged groups. Despite confronting challenges because of his color and sexual orientation, he persisted in his resolve to change the industry and use his platform to advance social justice, accountability, and transparency.

Relationships And Family

Don Lemon is a quiet individual when it comes to his relationships and personal life, yet he has disclosed certain information to the public. He has been in a serious relationship with Tim Malone, a realtor, since 2017, and he is openly gay.

Don Lemon

Tim Malone and Don Lemon wed in a private ceremony later that year after announcing their engagement in April 2019. On social media, they have posted pictures and information about their relationship, including their travels and adventures.

Leisa and Yma, two older sisters, make up Don Lemon's family. He has discussed his family's influence on his life and profession as well as their relationship in public. He attributes his strong work ethic and dedication to social justice to his mother, who passed away in 2018.

Don Lemon has likewise been transparent about his battles with alcoholism and has discussed his choice to quit drinking. He has emphasized the value of getting treatment and assistance for addiction and has urged others who might be experiencing addiction to follow his example.

Even though Don Lemon keeps his personal life private, he has talked about his relationships and family in some

Don Lemon

depth. He has spoken openly about his sober path, the value of getting support, and has given his family credit for helping to mold who he is now.

.

CHAPTER 2: CAREER AS A JOURNALIST

Don Lemon is a renowned journalist and television news host who is well-known for his in-depth reporting on breaking news stories and his provocative commentary on social and political topics. In New York City, where he started his media career as a news assistant, he went on to work as a reporter and news anchor for a number of regional news outlets across the country.

Don Lemon became a journalist for CNN in 2006 and has since covered a wide range of domestic and international issues, such as Hurricane Katrina, the Haitian earthquake, and the Gulf oil spill. Later, he was given the opportunity to anchor "CNN Newsroom," a weekend prime-time news program, and "CNN Tonight," a weekday prime-time news program.

Don Lemon

Don Lemon has covered some of the most important historical events as a news anchor and correspondent, including the 9/11 terrorist attacks, the Boston Marathon bombing, and the 2016 presidential election. He is well regarded for his capacity to offer perceptive and considerate criticism on difficult subjects, and he has won numerous honors and accolades for his journalism work.

Don Lemon has consistently used his platform to campaign for social justice and equality, bringing attention to problems like racial injustice, police brutality, and LGBTQ rights. He has received honors for his advocacy work, including the NABJ President's Award and the Walter Cronkite Award for Excellence in Journalism, for his initiatives to advance diversity and inclusion in the media sector.

Don Lemon has generally had a prestigious career as a journalist and news anchor, covering some of the most important events of our time and speaking out for key social concerns. He is a renowned and significant person

Don Lemon

in the field of media thanks to his intelligent analysis and commitment to truth and honesty.

Approach To Journalism And His Thoughts On The Future Of Media.

Don Lemon has been a journalist and newscaster for CNN since 2006. He employs a distinctive style of journalism that emphasizes candor and expressing one's thoughts without fear. He thinks that journalists should utilize their platforms to advocate for social change and that they shouldn't be afraid to express their opinions on topics that are important to them.

Don Lemon's willingness to speak out on social and political issues that he is passionate about is one of the defining characteristics of his approach to journalism. He has, for instance, been outspoken in his criticism of the Trump administration and in his opposition to racism, homophobia, and other types of discrimination. His platform has been used to advance understanding and acceptance of people from various backgrounds and identities. He has also been a voice for the LGBTQ+ community.

Don Lemon has worked as a journalist and news caster, but he has also been a vocal supporter of media innovation. With the rise of digital media and the waning influence of traditional news channels, he thinks the business is changing. He has claimed that adopting new platforms and technology is crucial for the future of journalism, and that in order for journalists to remain useful and effective, they must be prepared to change.

Don Lemon has also made statements regarding the value of inclusivity and diversity in the media sector. He has stated that news companies ought to do more to recruit and advance journalists from a variety of backgrounds and to give people of different racial, gender, and sexual orientations the chance to express their opinions. Additionally, he has pushed for increased accountability and transparency in the media and

Don Lemon

challenged journalists to be open and truthful with their audiences.

Overall, honesty, ethics, and a commitment to social justice define Don Lemon's journalism style. According to him, journalists have a duty to be honest and upfront with their viewers as well as to use their platforms to encourage social change. He also acknowledges that the media landscape is changing and that for journalists to be effective and relevant in the coming years, they must be open to embracing new technology and platforms.

CHAPTER 3: CAREER AS A NEWS ASSISTANT AT WNYW

When Don Lemon was hired as a news assistant at WNYW in New York City in 1991, his career in journalism officially got underway. Lemon played a behind-the-scenes role in assisting news reporters and producers in gathering and reporting news stories. Lemon immediately won over his colleagues with his work ethic and obvious flair for journalism despite his entry-level position.

Lemon was given the chance to serve as a weekend anchor and general assignment reporter at the station after a few years of working as a news assistant. He covered a variety of stories in this capacity, from breaking news to feature articles. He also started to establish his on-air persona, becoming renowned for his measured, calm delivery and propensity for challenging listeners.

Don Lemon

Lemon changed careers in 1999, taking a position as a correspondent for NBC News in Chicago. In this capacity, he covered a variety of domestic and international topics, including the explosion in Oklahoma City, the O.J. Simpson trial, and Princess Diana's passing. He also did a lot of traveling, reporting from places like Nigeria, Pakistan, and Afghanistan.

In the industry, Lemon became well-known and respected for his work at NBC News. He was well-known for his prowess in interviewing newsmakers and experts as well as for his capacity to cover breaking news events from the scene. Nevertheless, despite his success, Lemon started to feel as though he wasn't making the most of his platform to address the issues that most concerned him.

Lemon decided to transfer to CNN in 2006 because he believed he could have a bigger impact there on advocacy and journalism. His choice would prove to be a turning point in his professional life, catapulting him to even greater levels of success and prominence in the field.

Lemon gained a great understanding of how the media can affect public perception and the course of events through his experience covering significant news events like the O.J. Simpson trial and the Oklahoma City bombing. He gained a strong appreciation for the value of objectivity and accuracy in reporting from this experience, and he vowed to use his platform to advance accountability and openness.

Lemon believed he could do more to address the issues that most concerned him, despite his success as a correspondent at NBC News. He was particularly worried about the media's lack of diversity and the manner in which it can reinforce negative assumptions and biases.

Lemon has had the opportunity to confront these problems head-on at CNN, where he has been able to use his platform to promote social justice and question the established quo. He has gained notoriety for his blunt criticism on racial, sexual, and social justice issues and has won praise for his dedication to advancing openness and responsibility in the media.

Overall, Don Lemon's time working as a news assistant at WNYW in the beginning of his career and his move to becoming an NBC News reporter helped him get the knowledge and experience required to become one of the most renowned and powerful journalists in the business. His choice to join CNN gave him the opportunity to fully utilize his platform to speak out on the subjects that most concerned him and promote social justice, openness, and accountability in the media.

Move To Cnn And Rise To Prominence As A News Anchor And Host

Don Lemon decided to switch from NBC News to CNN in 2006. He was initially employed as a news anchor and correspondent, but it didn't take him long to advance through the network's ranks.

When Lemon was one of the top reporters covering Barack Obama's historic presidential campaign in 2008, it was one of his first significant moments at CNN. Lemon swiftly rose to the position of one of CNN's most recognizable political faces as a result of the depth and insight of his reporting, which received high accolades.

Don Lemon has anchored a variety of CNN programs throughout the years, such as "CNN Tonight with Don Lemon," "CNN Newsroom," and "CNN Special Investigations Unit." Additionally, he has worked as a correspondent for the network, reporting on breaking news stories both domestically and abroad.

Lemon's singular viewpoint on the world has played a significant role in his ascent to fame as a news anchor and host. He is renowned for his willingness to tackle challenging subjects and pose challenging queries, even when they are unpopular or divisive. He is renowned for speaking up on matters of race, sexuality, and social justice. He has also received praise for his dedication to fostering openness and responsibility in the media.

The news sector has been significantly impacted by Lemon. As a result of his talent for relating to audiences and demystifying complex topics in a way that is both educational and entertaining, he has emerged as one of the most well-known and respected journalists in the nation. Additionally, he has been a steadfast supporter of diversity and inclusion in the media, utilizing his platform to emphasize the value of representation and refute unfavorable assumptions and biases.

Don Lemon's career at CNN experienced one of its defining moments following the police shooting of Michael Brown in Ferguson, Missouri, in 2014. Lemon went to Ferguson to cover the demonstrations and disturbances that occurred after the shooting, and his reporting was hailed for its breadth and depth.

Don Lemon

Lemon made waves when he sadly described his own experiences with prejudice and discrimination during his coverage of the Ferguson protests. His moving on-air speech connected with viewers and sparked a wider discussion on racial equity and social justice in the US.

Since then, Lemon has continued to use his position at CNN as a platform to promote social justice and refute damaging assumptions and biases. He routinely calls for more openness and accountability in law enforcement and has been particularly outspoken on issues involving racial profiling and police brutality.

However, there has been some controversy around Lemon's commentary. His strong opinions on political subjects, particularly his criticism of former President Donald Trump, have drawn condemnation from some quarters. Lemon has persisted in his resolve to use his platform to advance openness, responsibility, and social justice despite this criticism.

Don Lemon

Don Lemon's career at CNN has generally been characterized by his readiness to tackle difficult subjects and challenge the status quo. His distinctive viewpoint and steadfast dedication to advancing openness, accountability, and social justice have made him one of the most well-known and respected journalists in the business.

CHAPTER 4: COVERAGE OF MAJOR NEWS EVENTS

Don Lemon's coverage of significant news events in the United States and around the world has come to define his career as a journalist. Here are some instances of his noteworthy reporting:

Katrina the hurricane

Don Lemon was one of the first reporters on the scene in New Orleans after Hurricane Katrina in 2005. He provided live coverage from the destroyed city, capturing the mayhem and devastation brought on by the storm as well as the shortcomings of the government's reaction. His reportage aided in drawing attention to the disaster's human toll and the structural problems that contributed to the government's ineffective reaction.

Don Lemon

bombing at the Boston Marathon:

Don Lemon was one of the main reporters reporting the Boston Marathon bombing in 2013, which resulted in three fatalities and hundreds of injuries. He provided updates during the suspects' manhunt while reporting live from the bombing scene. His reporting aided in giving viewers a good grasp of the developing scenario and the efforts being made by the police to apprehend the offenders.

American presidential election, 2016:

Don Lemon was a strident opponent of Donald Trump during the 2016 U.S. presidential election. He refuted Trump's assertions and offered a thorough examination of the election's key problems. After Trump's victory, Lemon continued to critique the president's policies and deeds, regularly refuting his claims and holding him responsible for his choices.

Don Lemon

The presidential election of 2008:

Lemon covered Barack Obama's historic election as the nation's first Black president in-depth, examining how his triumph would affect racial tensions and politics in the nation.

the Ebola epidemic

Lemon covered the Ebola outbreak in West Africa in depth in 2014, emphasizing the disease's catastrophic effects on local people and the international reaction to the catastrophe.

The 2016 mass shooting at the Pulse nightclub in Orlando, Florida, resulted in 49 fatalities and several injuries. Don Lemon was there to cover the event. His coverage contributed to a better understanding of the victims and the community's reaction to the tragedy.

Don Lemon has been an outspoken supporter of the Black Lives Matter movement, covering demonstrations and advocacy campaigns against racial inequality and police brutality. He has spoken with activists and subject matter specialists and given a forum to perspectives frequently left out of mainstream media.

Don Lemon has established a reputation for providing serious analysis, in-depth reporting, and a willingness to tackle difficult subjects through his coverage of these and other events. He has established himself as a reliable and well-respected journalist who is dedicated to using his platform to advance social justice and transparency in the media.

Involvement In The Black Lives Matter Movement

On and off the air, Don Lemon has actively supported the Black Lives Matter movement. He participated in a protest march in June 2020 in New York City, where he resides and works. He has additionally promoted Black activists' views and amplified their voices on social media platforms.

Don Lemon has underlined the value of nonviolent protest in his coverage of the demonstrations and has denounced those who resort to violence and mayhem. Additionally, he has advocated for increased understanding and compassion between law enforcement and the communities they serve, and he has urged both parties to participate in communication and work toward improvement.

Many people have commended Don Lemon's reporting on the Black Lives Matter movement and the demonstrations that followed George Floyd's passing for being insightful and nuanced. The 2020 Edward R. Murrow Award for his reporting on institutional racism in America is only one of the accolades he has received for his coverage of these topics.

Don Lemon came out against police violence and demanded structural reform in response to the racial

Don Lemon

disparity problems in America after Floyd's passing. He
interviewed activists and community leaders who were
trying to bring about significant change, and he offered
in-depth coverage of the protests that took place in
places all throughout the United States.

Don Lemon has shown a dedication to using his platform
to advance social justice and equality by his participation
in the Black Lives Matter movement and his reporting
on the demonstrations and public turmoil that followed
the killing of George Floyd. His reporting has been a
potent force in bringing these crucial concerns to light
and in advocating for significant change in American
society.

CHAPTER 5: ADVOCACY FOR SOCIAL JUSTICE

Don Lemon is a well-known supporter of social justice who has utilized his position as a journalist to raise awareness of topics including racism, police brutality, and the rights of LGBTQ+ people. He has repeatedly reported stories about these concerns, including high-profile examples of police shootings, and has been a prominent critic of institutional racism and police violence against people of color.

Lemon has also been a steadfast supporter of LGBTQ+ rights and has utilized his own experiences as a homosexual man to spread awareness of the bigotry and discrimination that the LGBTQ+ community must endure. He has advocated strongly for marriage equality and other LGBTQ+ rights issues and has spoken out against anti-LGBTQ+ laws and practices.

Don Lemon

Lemon has been part in advocacy work to advance social justice and equality in addition to reporting on these subjects. He has collaborated with groups like the National Association of Black Journalists and the Human Rights Campaign to advance inclusion and diversity in the media sector and to support laws that defend vulnerable groups.

Don Lemon has established himself as a strong advocate for social justice and equality in the media sector through his reporting and advocacy activities. He has made use of his platform to draw attention to the struggles of underrepresented groups and to encourage empathy and deeper understanding among his audience. His work has motivated others to take action and get involved in advocacy initiatives aimed at promoting social justice and equality and has assisted in drawing attention to important topics such as racism, police brutality, and LGBTQ+ rights.

Don Lemon

Contributions To Lgbtq+ Advocacy

Throughout his career, Don Lemon has been a prominent supporter of LGBTQ+ rights, both on and off the air. He has spoken for issues affecting the LGBTQ+ community, including assault, harassment, and prejudice, using his platform as a journalist and news anchor.

Numerous organizations and advocacy groups have honored Lemon for his services to the LGBTQ+ movement. The Human Rights Campaign, the largest LGBTQ+ advocacy group in the US, gave him the Visibility Award in 2011. The honor is granted each year to someone who has significantly aided the cause of LGBTQ+ visibility and rights.

Lemon discussed his own experiences as a gay man, the difficulties he has had in both his personal and professional life, in accepting the prize. Additionally, he underlined the significance of using one's platform to speak out in favor of social justice and equality and

Don Lemon

urged others to join him in supporting causes that advance the rights and visibility of LGBTQ+ people.

Throughout his career, both on and off the air, Lemon has continued to serve as an advocate. He has defended same-sex unions and spoken out against violence and bigotry aimed at the LGBTQ+ community. Additionally, he has pushed for more LGBTQ+ people to be represented in the media and urged media outlets to be more accepting and helpful to LGBTQ+ journalists and staff.

Don Lemon has made a sizable and varied contribution to LGBTQ+ advocacy overall. Through his advocacy activities, he has aided in bringing attention to the struggles faced by the LGBTQ+ community and has prompted his coworkers and viewers to show more empathy and compassion. The fact that the Human Rights Campaign has recognized him speaks volumes about the influence of his work and the significance of promoting social justice and equality for all.

CHAPTER 6: LEMON'S PERSONAL EXPERIENCES WITH RACISM AND HOMOPHOBIA

Don Lemon's activism efforts and journalism have been significantly influenced by his personal experiences with racism and homophobia. Lemon has experienced prejudice and discrimination throughout his life as a Black man and member of the LGBTQ+ community, and these experiences have influenced his reporting and advocacy work.

Lemon experienced personally the consequences of institutionalized racism and segregation while growing up in Louisiana. He has talked openly about his encounters with racism, including instances in which he was subjected to racial epithets and harsh treatment because of his race. His journalistic platform has given him the opportunity to spotlight underrepresented communities' struggles and to speak out in favor of laws

Don Lemon

that advance social justice and equality. These experiences have inspired him to do so.

Lemon has also been transparent about his encounters with homophobia and his choice to come out as gay in 2011. He has been a steadfast supporter of LGBTQ+ rights and has utilized his platform to increase public awareness of the bigotry and discrimination that the LGBTQ+ community must contend with. He has been a strong advocate for marriage equality and other LGBTQ+ rights issues and has been a prominent opponent of anti-LGBTQ+ laws and policies.

Don Lemon's journalism and advocacy efforts have been significantly influenced by these personal experiences. Using his platform to expose the stories of people of color and the LGBTQ+ community and to encourage more understanding and empathy among his viewers, he has been a powerful advocate for disadvantaged communities. His work has encouraged others to take part in advocacy campaigns that support social justice and equality.

Don Lemon

Don Lemon has utilized his personal experiences to advocate for more diversity and inclusion in the media profession in addition to his reporting and advocacy efforts. He has worked with groups like the National Association of Black Journalists and the Human Rights Campaign to advance these initiatives. He has been a major supporter of increased representation of people of color and LGBTQ+ people in newsrooms.

Lemon has also been a vocal opponent of the media industry's lack of diversity and has advocated for greater representation in front of and behind the camera. He has urged people to support media organizations that place a high priority on diversity and inclusiveness as well as called on media firms to increase their commitment to these ideals.

In 2020, Lemon made an emotional on-air appeal for more empathy and understanding among Americans in reaction to the widespread protests that followed the death of George Floyd. He addressed white Americans specifically, pleading with them to acknowledge their privilege and pay attention to the realities of people of color. The video's strong message caused it to become popular and receive much accolades.

In general, Don Lemon's personal encounters with racism and homophobia have had a big impact on his advocacy work and journalism. His position has been used to promote greater diversity, inclusion, and empathy in the media sector as well as in American culture at large. He has also raised awareness of prejudice and discrimination. His contributions have had a long-lasting influence on American media and have encouraged others to participate in advocacy campaigns for social justice and equality.

CHAPTER 7: DON LEMON'S BOOK "TRANSPARENT" AND ITS IMPACT ON DISCUSSIONS OF RACE AND SEXUALITY IN THE MEDIA

The memoir "Transparent" by Don Lemon delves at the intersections of his conflicting identities—race and sexuality—and how they have affected his life and work. The book, which was released in 2011, not long after Lemon came out as gay, had a big impact on how people talked about race and sexuality in the media.

Lemon is open about his encounters with racism and homophobia in "Transparent," as well as how they have impacted his personal and professional life. He talks about his desire to come out as gay and the difficulties he encountered doing so as a well-known person. He also considers his experiences as a Black journalist and how his race has affected his reporting and how his coworkers and audience members regard him.

Don Lemon

The book has received appreciation for its candid and accurate depiction of Lemon's personal experiences as well as for its contribution to topics of race and sexuality in the media. By telling his story, Lemon has inspired greater empathy and understanding among his readers and helped to increase awareness of the difficulties faced by people of color and LGBTQ+ persons in the media sector.

Discussions of diversity and inclusion in media more generally have been influenced by "Transparent" as well. The book has been used in talks about the need for more representation of people of color and LGBTQ+ persons in newsrooms and media organizations, as well as being utilized as a teaching resource in journalism and media studies schools.

"Transparent" has been lauded for its potent message about the value of sincerity and honesty in addition to its influence on media topics of race and sexuality. Lemon stresses the necessity of being authentic and leading a life that is consistent with one's principles and views throughout the entire book. He exhorts readers to be truthful with both themselves and other people, despite trying circumstances or social pressure to fit in.

Readers from various walks of life have found this message to be relevant, and it has encouraged others to pursue lives that are more sincere and honest. Lemon has received acclaim for his boldness in speaking up about the struggles marginalized communities experience in the media industry and beyond, as well as for his bravery in sharing his own personal narrative.

In addition, "Transparent" has received praise for being easy to read and understand. Lemon's voice is appealing and accessible, and the book is written in a conversational tone. This has made the book more approachable to a variety of readers and expanded the discussion regarding race, sexuality, and identity in media.

Overall, "Transparent" has significantly influenced how race and sexuality are discussed in the media and has supported the development of a more diverse and equal media environment. Don Lemon has shared his personal narrative and increased understanding of the struggles faced by underrepresented groups in the media profession and beyond through the publication of his memoir. He has motivated people to join advocacy campaigns that support social justice and equality, and he has urged readers to be more genuine and honest in their own lives.

Lemon's Thoughts On The Importance Of Transparency And Accountability In The Media.

Don Lemon has made numerous speeches emphasizing the value of accountability and openness in the media. According to him, journalists have a duty to be truthful and open with their readers and to hold both themselves and other people accountable for their deeds.

Don Lemon

Being forthright and honest about his personal prejudices and viewpoints is one way Don Lemon encourages media honesty. Everyone has biases, he has said, and in order to report fairly and accurately, journalists need to be conscious of their own biases.

Don Lemon has also been outspoken in his criticism of false information and fake news, which he believes can have a negative effect on democracy and public dialogue. He urged reporters to conduct fact checks on their reports and to be open and honest about their sources and reporting techniques.

Don Lemon has been a steadfast supporter of the First Amendment and press freedom in addition to advocating for transparency and accountability in the media. He has spoken out against attacks on media organizations and journalists, and he has underlined the significance of safeguarding journalists' freedom to cover significant stories without fear of reprisal or censorship.

Don Lemon

Overall, according to Don Lemon, the public's trust in journalism and the media's ability to serve the public interest depend on transparency and accountability. He has advocated for these principles and urged other journalists to follow suit by using his platform.

Don Lemon

Don Lemon's role as a mentor to young journalists and his efforts to promote diversity in media.

Don Lemon has been a steadfast supporter of increasing media diversity and has actively participated in mentoring aspiring journalists from underrepresented groups. He has advocated for better representation of women, people of color, and LGBTQ+ people in the media and pushed to provide these people the tools they need to be successful in the field of journalism.

Don Lemon has taken up a mentoring role for aspiring journalists as part of his initiatives to advance diversity in the media. He has helped emerging journalists, particularly those from marginalized groups, by offering direction, counsel, and support. Young journalists have been urged by him to utilize their platforms to advocate for social change and to speak out on causes that are important to them.

Along with his mentoring initiatives, Don Lemon has actively promoted inclusivity and diversity in

Don Lemon

newsrooms. He has pushed news companies to do more to recruit and advance journalists from a variety of backgrounds and to foster an inclusive and welcoming workplace environment for all staff members.

Don Lemon has also actively participated in initiatives that support media diversity. For instance, he has mentored students through the National Association of Black Journalists' student mentoring program and the International Women's Media Foundation. He has also given a keynote address at the Excellence in Journalism conference, where he has spoken to aspiring journalists about his perspectives and experiences.

Overall, Don Lemon's mentoring and advocacy work have greatly aided in the advancement of inclusivity and diversity in the media. He has inspired young journalists to follow their passions and change the world by using his position to open doors for underrepresented communities.

CHAPTER 8: INVOLVEMENT IN PHILANTHROPIC WORK

Throughout his professional life, Don Lemon has been actively involved in philanthropic activity and has given to numerous charitable organizations. He has advocated for causes that he is passionate about by using his platform as a journalist and news anchor to bring attention to significant social challenges.

The LGBTQ+ community is one of the subjects Don Lemon has taken a particular interest in. His platform has been used to advance understanding and acceptance of persons of all sexual orientations and gender identities. He has been an advocate for LGBTQ+ rights. Numerous LGBTQ+ groups, such as the National Lesbian and Gay Journalists Association and the Hetrick-Martin Institute, which offers assistance to LGBTQ+ kids, are affiliated with him.

Don Lemon

Don Lemon has also been active in anti-HIV and anti-AIDS groups. He has participated in activities to spread awareness about the effects of HIV/AIDS on communities all over the world and has supported the AIDS Healthcare Foundation, which offers HIV/AIDS testing, treatment, and advocacy services.

Don Lemon has sponsored other philanthropic projects in addition to his work with groups that serve LGBTQ+ and HIV/AIDS patients. He has worked with the Harlem School of the Arts, which offers arts education programs for students in impoverished regions, as well as the Boys and Girls Clubs of America, which offers after-school activities and mentoring services for young people.

Overall, Don Lemon's participation in charitable endeavors has served as evidence of his dedication to having a beneficial impact on the world. He has relentlessly worked to help groups that are improving people's lives all around the world and has utilized his position to spread awareness of significant social concerns.

Don Lemon

Participation In Community Outreach Programs

Throughout his career, Don Lemon has actively participated in community engagement initiatives and put a lot of work into supporting his hometown. He has advocated for good change in the areas where he lives and works by using his platform as a journalist and news anchor to bring attention to significant social concerns.

Don Lemon's work with the Boys and Girls Clubs of America is one way he has given back to his community. He has represented the group as a spokesperson and taken part in fundraising activities to promote its services and initiatives. Additionally, he has collaborated with the Harlem School of the Arts, which offers arts education programs to pupils in impoverished areas, and he has been a steadfast supporter of expanding all children's access to high-quality education.

Don Lemon has taken part in local community projects and events in addition to his work with organizations. He

Don Lemon

has taken part in charity races and walks to raise money for a variety of causes, such as HIV/AIDS awareness and education, and he has been an outspoken supporter of LGBTQ+ rights in his neighborhood. He has also advocated for the need to encourage startups and small enterprises by working with neighborhood businesses and organizations to promote economic growth.

Overall, Don Lemon's involvement in charitable initiatives and efforts to support his hometown have played a significant role in his career as a journalist and campaigner. He has relentlessly worked to assist groups and programs that are improving the lives of people in his town and beyond and has utilized his position to spread awareness about crucial social concerns.

CHAPTER 9: RECOGNITION AND AWARDS FOR HIS JOURNALISM AND ADVOCACY WORK

Throughout his career, Don Lemon has been honored and recognized with various accolades for his advocacy work and services to journalism. Here are a few of his noteworthy honors and commendations:

- Emmy Award: Don Lemon has received numerous Emmy Awards for his services as a news anchor and journalist over the course of his career. His reporting and coverage of breaking news events have earned him numerous other honors since he won his first Emmy in 2002 for his coverage of the capture of the D.C. area sniper.

- Don Lemon won the Edward R. Murrow Award in 2009 for his reporting on the arrest of the "Craigslist Killer" in Boston.

Don Lemon

- GLAAD Award: Don Lemon has won a number of GLAAD Awards for his work as an LGBTQ+ community advocate. He received the Vito Russo Award in 2014, which is given to a media practitioner who is openly LGBTQ+ and has made a major contribution to the advancement of equality and acceptance.

- 2019 National Association of Black Journalists (NABJ) Journalist of the Year: Don Lemon received this honor from the NABJ in 2019. The honor highlighted both his journalistic efforts and his support of diversity and inclusiveness in the media.

- Don Lemon was given the NAACP President's Award in 2020, which honors people who have significantly contributed to the cause of social justice and equality.

- Don Lemon has been named several times, including in 2014 and 2020, to TIME magazine's annual list of the 100 most influential people.

- Emmy for Outstanding Long Form Live Coverage of a Current News Story: For his coverage of the 2018 Pittsburgh synagogue shooting, Don Lemon won an Emmy Award in 2020. For several hours, he served as the host of CNN's live coverage of the event. He also offered breaking news updates all day long.

- Don Lemon has won numerous Gracie Awards, which honor exceptional programs produced by women in the media. In 2014, he was recognized with the Gracie Award for Outstanding Interview for his discussion with Rachel Jeantel, a pivotal witness in the George Zimmerman prosecution.

- Don Lemon was given the National Headliner Award in 2014 for his coverage of the Boston Marathon bombing.

Don Lemon

- Don Lemon won the 2017 Walter Cronkite Award for Excellence in Journalism in recognition of his achievements in journalism and his support of social justice.

- Don Lemon was given the NABJ President's Award in 2018 for his support of inclusion and diversity in the media sector.

- Don Lemon won a Telly Award in 2020 for his reporting on COVID-19's effects on Black Americans.

The honors and accolades Don Lemon has received demonstrate both his commitment to and achievements in the area of journalism as well as his support for significant social causes. He has received praise for covering breaking news stories, conducting important interview subjects' interviews, and working to advance diversity and inclusion in the media.

CONCLUSION

Don Lemon is a well-known journalist and television news host who has a successful career in journalism. He has covered some of the most important events of our time and fought for key social causes. He has received praise for his perceptive criticism, commitment to honesty and openness, and determination to advancing social justice and equality.

Don Lemon has fought arduously for increased representation for marginalized groups throughout his career and has been an outspoken proponent of diversity and inclusion in the media. He has also been a steadfast supporter of the Black Lives Matter movement, using his platform to bring attention to problems involving institutional racism and police brutality.

In addition to his work as a journalist, Don Lemon is active in philanthropy and has donated a substantial amount of money to numerous nonprofits. He is dedicated to cultivating the next group of media industry leaders and serves as a mentor to young journalists.

Lemon's commitment to truth, openness, and social fairness is demonstrated by his life and career. His work has had a significant impact on how we comprehend and interact with some of the most significant challenges affecting our society today. He has been a significant voice in American journalism.

Made in the USA
Monee, IL
11 November 2023

46245374R00033